To Brad
Happy Gardening!
Cheryl Jacques

The Magnolia Principle:

How Seeds, Weeds and Needs Bloom Inner Peace

Cheryl Jacques

AuthorHouse™
1663 Liberty Drive
Bloomington, IN 47403
www.authorhouse.com
Phone: 1-800-839-8640

First published by AuthorHouse 2/2/2010

ISBN: 978-1-4490-7736-5 (sc)

Library of Congress Control Number: 2010901057

Printed in the United States of America
Bloomington, Indiana

This book is printed on acid-free paper.

This book is dedicated to

my best friend Amie Thornburg and my loving husband Ron.

Amie, our marathon conversations at Carnegies, our frivolous trips to see Rick Springfield, and our countless email conversations have been the most fulfilling experiences of my life. Best friends like you only come around once in a lifetime. Thanks for listening......

Ron, how lucky to have married a man who will accompany two girlfriends to see numerous Rick Springfield concerts without complaint, a man who allows me the time to have four hour dinners with her best friend, and a man who has supported every silly dream I've ever entertained.

Thank you for all your words of wisdom and your passion for life.

John Stilgoe, Robert and Lois Orchard Professor in the History of Landscape at the Visual and Environmental Studies Department of Harvard University is the author of many award winning books such as *Borderland: Origins of the American Suburb 1820-1939, Outside Lies Magic,* and most recently *Train Time: Railroads and Imminent Landscape Change.*

He's also been featured in a *60 Minutes* episode entitled "The Eyes Have It" about his inspiring and eccentric way of teaching his students to get out of the classroom and to "look around" at the built environment. A teacher at Harvard since 1977, Professor Stilgoe has captured the hearts and minds of his students and continues to inspire.

Foreword:

Read this floral philosophy and free yourself of electronic foolery. Today we slog through digital information but find little meaning. The Internet overwhelms and makes too much too easy. Software skews learning. Not long ago when unsure of how to spell a word, we looked in dictionaries, and to our surprise found words we did not know. Now software checks our spelling and sends us the news stories it thinks we want to read. The newspaper alerted us to news we did not imagine but might find useful, even if only to stretch our minds. But gardening is different from virtual reality, so different we forget to realize why we love it so.

In this book blossoms some plant-centered philosophy. Eminently sensible, provocative, and immediately useful, *The Magnolia Principle* analyzes attitudes expressed via plants and offers an escape from computer-generated buzziness. In these pages plants take on alternative meaning.

Here plants become portal. The principle of the title emphasizes choice, the choice to look around positively, accepting some loss in exchange for some gain, but always with the intention (and the hope) that gain will triumph. A magnolia might bloom many times in Indiana before a frost prevents the beauty. Why not plant it and risk the occasional loss for the intermittent splendor? Why not look at plants and also *through* them, through plants as portal to philosophy?

Wisteria triumphs only slowly, as its roots reach deeply: years later, pruning the roots with a spade often produces spectacular blossoming. Hydrangeas need water, lots of water, at first: they need a patient gardener, one willing to water regularly and frequently and munificently. Rhododendrons too can and will triumph in Indiana soils and microclimates and as this book makes clear, Lucifer plants will bloom adjacent to a church. Knowledge proves a necessity, but gardener attitude may be more important and portal and attitude change together in ways that shape larger life.

In the pages that follow Cheryl Jacques walks carefully through that portal, guiding the reader into the philosophy suffusing plants, a philosophy especially valuable in this hurried, jittery age. The magnolia principle illuminates friendship, aging, illness, disability, energy, determination, and the sheer joy that plants provide when gardeners see past their frustrations and vexations through the portal plants provide. Here find a modest book whose meaning is rare and lasting.

John R. Stilgoe
Professor of Landscape Architecture
Harvard University

Table of Contents

Setting Up...

This early morning before the Indianapolis Flower and Patio Show opens, amid the dust of other landscape contractors' earthy debris, I'm carefully attending to the myriad details involved in finishing set-up of my own Tuscan inspired garden.

As I work I'm relishing the odors of fresh plants bursting into full glory, mingled with those of soil, decayed mulch and freshly-sawed wood. I grew up in a nursery family (with Indiana nursery roots going way back into the 1800s; I was born in Cambridge City, and I now live just 45 minutes away in Greenfield, right next to the birthplace of the famed "Hoosier Poet," James Whitcomb Riley); and I eventually took a Master's degree in Landscape Architecture at Harvard University. And I've never been the least bit bored with the threads of nature I use to design and nurture my multi-dimensioned "life weavings" of color, texture, odor and form.

Surrounded as I was when a child, by 450 acres of flourishing crabapples, pears, maples, evergreens and blossoming viburnum, my spirit bears an indelible mark Nature left on me. In fact, I never knew a time when I wasn't surrounded by growing things. Most of my days were spent out in the fields, armed with an old-fashioned walkie-talkie, an army-style canteen and a sketchpad on which I could indulge my fascination with flowers, plants and trees.

I remember in Spring I'd try to time the falling of pink crabapple flowers just right, when they'd drift like pink, effervescent snow. The petals would shed to make way for the leaves, and to bask underneath a "snowing" tree, "showering" in the petals, was for me like sheer heaven.

For a while after I got my first, undergraduate degree in landscape architecture, I was tempted to study building-architecture – some people told me I couldn't "reach my full potential" if I stayed in landscape architecture. They claimed building-architecture was "The Mother of All Arts."

But I decided that Nature was the true Mother of All Arts, and I realized that most of the building-architects I admired strongest had sought hardest to abstract Nature's essence in their designs. So I went to Harvard to pursue my Master's in Landscape Architecture, from 1990-1992.

Afterwards, my upbringing's deep roots pulled me back to Indiana, where I opened my own nursery, landscape design and residential master planning firm. I craved open space and fields, and yes, even weeds and the chance to develop my own style – to create little pieces of "Arcadia" (that's what I've called our nursery) in smaller prototypes, to help people open their senses and spirits, live more fully and understand… not so much the "*how*-to's" and even "*why*-to's," but more crucially the "why-*for's*" of gardening. That I'm sometimes able to share that insight has been my measure of success, and I think my great-grandfather and other forebears would be happy with it.

So is my husband, Ron, who's as always helping me set up. He comes near me now, smiling radiantly, his face and hair spattered with mud clumps and flecks of paint from installing the structure. I jest that he looks like a walking Jackson Pollock canvas (he admires that painter most)

"So, what to do you think?" he grins, gazing around.

I should let "reality" temper my excitement – this is a huge aesthetic, philosophical and emotional investment for us – but I blurt out, "I think it's our best garden yet!" I return his knowing, appreciative glance and put my loamy hand in his for an impetuous little squeeze as we survey the sweep of our garden-in-progress.

A constructed wall that resembles the courtyard of a formal piazza borders its longest side complete with a clay tile roof. I've also incorporated a formal wrought iron fence and boxwood hedge to front its "public" side, to create little plant niches that break up the length of the space visually. Oregano, parsley, and creeping thyme along the edges of the simulated courtyard will complete the authenticity of the Tuscan planting palette.

Now Ron's walking me through the rest of the layout to help me make fully sure it realizes what I've drawn on paper. I see that the enclosures of both natural and man-made elements do achieve their purposes exactly as I intended, to create a sense of serene seclusion from the hurly-burly of the Show.

I hope at least some who enter this environment will understand the "language" I want it to speak, and I envision the hours and the people soon to come...

Surging masses of humanity will traipse in and out of my garden space, holding brightly colored drink cups, holding stacks of business cards and flyers collected from every hopeful vendor here. And I wonder: Will there be some – any – among these crowds whose visions truly vibrate with this earth-rooted, life-weave of plants, stone, soil, water, metal and light it's been my craft, art and passion to create?

Will any I encounter realize not just *that*, but also *how* the things I've planted, nurtured and arranged mean more than mere creation of illustrative effects? Will some feel and resonate with the eloquent varieties life forms and forces that make up the whole harmonies of sight, scent, substance and sense I weave from Nature?

And will I find it possible to meld these vital threads with the particular personalities and quirks of the people I weave gardens for, so I and they might grasp the qualities and care needs of the plants and other highly diverse elements I suggest would intertwine best with their souls, minds and bodies?

Will I share with anyone like my best friend (since 5th grade) Amie? She's suffered for over ten years with ALS (also known as Lou Gehrig's disease, it causes progressive, irreversible atrophy and paralysis of the body's muscles); yet though she's becoming increasingly weaker and immobile physically, she continues to grow in spirit ever more aware, vital and accepting of my work and my love of things that root, grow from and rest in earth.

I look forward to seeing Amie at this event. She typically comes on the last days of my shows, lifting my spirits every time with her upbeat attitude and truly grateful eyes. She makes it easy for me to forget about her impediments when we're together. Amie's confined to a wheelchair now, so I always design my gardens to be accessible either by ramps or bridges that gently flow through the garden spaces. (If I may, I'd like to share with you in this book snippets of e-mails we've sent back and forth.)

If Amie and other spirits like her will join us and take part in what I call **The Magnolia Principle**, this'll be a wonderful Show indeed!

What's **The Magnolia Principle**? Please let me take a few moments to explain this joyful concept for you.

The Magnolia Principle

"What would you think about having a Magnolia tree in your garden?" Do you know, I've found over the years I've been a landscape architect that I can learn much about people's expectations of Nature and their ability to deal with the challenges gardening presents by asking questions as simple that one.

And I've found that people's answers to that particular question tend to fall one of two ways – one answer of which tells me whether they instinctively understand **The Magnolia Principle**.

The answerers I call **"Magnolia-Principled"** immediately share with joy their love for Magnolias as plants – for Magnolias' creamy white or pink flowers and pungent sweet fragrance. These people share with me how eagerly, if they had Magnolia trees in their gardens, they'd anticipate seeing the tree-buds' swell each year, to "announce" Spring's imminent arrival.

Their spirits make me smile instinctively.

The second answerers, though, immediately start to grouse about how early Spring killing frosts might nip off the Magnolia buds, or send flowers falling to the ground prematurely, to become drifts of "white leaf litter," as a responder like these frowned at me once.

About the second kind of responders I can't help thinking to myself, *What a shame, that they'd rather forego the likely ecstasies of seeing amazing Magnolia blossoms every Spring, just to avoid possible disappointment that might never even come!*

You see, **The Magnolia Principle** characterizes a spirit that can *embrace the coexistence of imperfections, strengths and beauties – in plants and in all of life.* This spirit accepts that not every Spring must have perfect weather. It nods gleefully at the impermanence of blossoms. It can even admire the powers of killing frosts.

The Magnolia Principle enjoys the labor of fertilizing and tendering contradictions together into wholes having parts that graciously enhance one another's beauties. It even smiles at the impertinence of weeds' carousing tries to confound a gardener's most careful designs.

The Magnolia Principle accepts that as you plan a garden, possible disappointment abounds everywhere! Your most intricate foreseeing care can only provide sketchy guidelines of the experience you'll have, because you may plant, you may build, you may tend to the soil, you may envision outcomes, but at day's end you realize you're only a servant of Nature, who's the true Architect.

And She and gardening can, if you let them, become among life's greatest Teachers, because both require patience that comes with the paradoxical certainty that you'll always be only so much in control of what you design.

Yet if you lend your energy to things, like Nature, bigger than yourself, and you let loose of all fear of disappointment, you can experience the possibility of tapping into the Universe – to see the twin melding of your aspirations with something that can't be fully controlled! You'll experience the fleeting joy of the Magnolia tree, the vivid anticipation of summer-blooming Daylilies and drink from Nature's ever-renewing fountain of inspiration and joy.

You'll grow a spirit like a surfer's who rides on the back of 20-foot swells, who can no more control the ocean than you can control Nature, so why try? Your spirit will toy with the possibility of the wipe-out, because you'll fully experience the ride, whatever its outcome.

I began learning **The Magnolia Principle** from my older brother, David, who died of leukemia when he was just 16, seven years older than I was then. Before he left us, as the disease weakened him into a wheelchair, David and my dad created a unique garden on the back patio for David to tend, which he did with consummate delight. I was privileged to help him in my small ways.

We built ramps and clusters of pots filled with every conceivable plant (in 139 separate containers!) for David to enjoy and care for, and I quickly came to love them, too. David's advancing disability seemed to fall away among the amazing growths and transformations that took place in that patio garden. Alongside him I learned how every tiny sprout, leaf and budding flower could emerge from all the complex genetic information coded in tiny seeds.

And as I worked with David and Dad, I absorbed things even more important: life principles of gratitude, patience, wonderment, living in the moment and acceptance – and I began learning how to tap into forces greater than myself that could help me grow and thrive, too.

I remember one time when David and I were expectantly watching carrots grow in one of the pots. David told me to be patient because they'd take longer to grow than other vegetables. But I was young and couldn't wait. When no one was around I dug one up – just an emaciated little root, really, at that point – ate it and then slyly tamped the earth down, hoping no one would notice I'd filched it.

Of course David soon after spotted the space my larceny had left and asked me if I'd sampled one of the fledgling carrots. I tried to swear up and down that I'd never touched one, but my dirt-covered face proclaimed me the culprit.

I finally fessed up that I'd indeed harvested the little carrot too early. I thought for sure David would be angry at me, but he wasn't. He smiled, "Cheryl, have you learned a lesson from what you did?" I said yes, and we laughed together.

Together David and I came to realize that understanding of all life could be found in those little pots, and I think that's why I decided to study landscape architecture. Not long after that, David, who'd gone improperly diagnosed for quite some time, contracted meningitis and became severely paralyzed almost overnight and died not long after. But what a living legacy he left me, as an older brother and a friend!

Now I have another best friend who can't move much at all any more, and it doesn't bother me in the slightest. Because I grew up with David, I see *Amie*, not her disability, and how how, despite her impediments, Amie seizes **The Magnolia Principle** with her whole soul: She even sees past the difficulties of her disease, to each day's precious gift of time in which she can move and laugh to any degree she's still able.

That's why I always hope that by the end of every garden show, Amie and I together – me with my expertise in Nature, and Amie with her joyful understanding of acceptance – will help many people discover **The Magnolia Principle**, not just for gardening, but for the whole of life. (I hope you'll learn a lot about it by reading and looking at this book.)

Spirits like Amie's, who already relish or can learn to relish **The Magnolia Principle**, are those I most want to share with at this Show. How many will I meet today? At least a few, I hope…

Now, as I work and meditate on my final touches to the garden, I'll give all my senses to finish weaving the varied living colors, odors, textures and meanings of some of the plants that comprise the palette of my design. Come, join me as I weave these delights into a magical vision of life!

"*Cheryl, you're right on the money with your Magnolia Principle! And as you probably could have guessed, I love Magnolias! In fact, I've always wanted one, so when you're placing your Spring order, if it's not too late, put an order in for me!*

"*I'm getting excited about planting some things now that the weather's getting better. I think I'm going to put in a fruit and small vegetable garden at the right end of the house by the driveway. Pat [Amie's husband] wants to put in a garden somewhere, but I think I'll put in some berries and such at the end of the house. Maybe we'll border it with some short privet hedges just at the curve of the drive, since that's where everyone drives into our yard anyway — maybe the privets will keep them in the driveway. I've ordered a couple of blueberry bushes and some strawberries, too. I'll make that my little area to mess around in.*

"*What do you think? Well, pencil me in for a couple of hours of coffee and talk someday soon!*"

(e-mail from Amie)

The Magnolia Tree: A Primal Plant

Why does it seem so very right to me to let **Magnolias** be my basis to assess people's attitudes about loving plants and meeting their needs? You may not know this, but Magnolias are ancient, almost primeval plants. Fossilized specimens of them have been found that date back more than 95 million years.

Magnolias apparently appeared on Earth even before bees did, so Magnolias don't blossom with distinct petals, like more modern flowers; they have more spatulate, tougher blooms called *tepals*, which apparently Nature designed to prevent the beetle species that first pollenated them from eating or damaging them.

Magnolias are for those who treasure primal things first…

Their beauty had to wait for eyes to evolve enough to see it. They clearly have possessed an amazing tenacity to survive the ages. Yet Magnolias' beginnings each Spring are fragile – so whoever loves them must also love delicacy.

For me the Magnolia Tree bursts with the fulness of potential Spring joy when its milky-white and pink blossoms emerge. My grandfather has a huge saucer Magnolia at his home, and as a little girl I liked to sit under its branches on windy days and let the blooms fall on me like fragrant, magical snow. And especially in early Spring, I'd try to imagine how the tree might have spent chilly night before…

The Magnolia's Song
To Endure Early Spring Frost

Shivering here in tonight's dark
I wish that streetlight across the way
could bleed heat like the sun.
So warm and lovely early Spring
beamed last afternoon, I just had
to open my buds to it in love.

Yes, I heard some man who walked
below me at twilight mutter,
"Magnolia, you've got false blossom-hopes;
by tomorrow, frost will leave you
without a petal on a branch."

Well, sir, my breed's been around
millions of years longer than yours,
and I'll prove you wrong!
I'll try to clutch my petals past dawn —
and even if I can't, I'll still
beat your chill by "snowing"
blooms all over you when you
walk by — see if I don't!

Wisterias, Time and Love

I don't think **Wisterias** are for people who think flowers appear instantaneously and by miracles. Most varieties of Wisteria take time and even root-pruning in order to speed up growth patterns – and even those varieties may take more than a half-dozen years to develop blooms. Against some gardeners' expectations, Wisterias require little fertilizing, and surprisingly, they develop better in gravelly soil. Ah, but when they explode, Wisteria trees plethora prolifically, their crowded blossoms often hanging down in huge bursts of spiraling glory I love to contemplate.

Wisterias spend their formative years expending most of their energy to produce new, unflowered growth, so at first they have very little pep left for blooming. Sort of like people, they have to establish themselves and understand who they are before they can flourish best.

Wisterias are members of the pea family, which form nitrogen-fixing nodules on their roots. That's why they don't need much fertilizing. In fact, if you over-fertilize them, they'll put out lots of vegetative growth, but *no* flowers. People who don't realize this have told me, "I don't know what's wrong with those Wisterias – I fertilize and fertilize them, and they never seem to flower!" Well, it was fertilizing them that *stunted* their flowering!

Wisteria to me symbolize patience and special love. A few varieties have been cultivated to bloom their first year, but many years of constant pruning and care may go into carefully training one small vine to burst with magnificent clusters of flowers that cascade down a large supportive trellis. So Wisteria's no plant for the faint of heart or someone who wants instant gratification. It may actually take a human lifetime or two to create a wisteria vine that's totally self-supportive, or one that creates its most spectacular show. You might even think of Wisteria as part of your legacy to a generation that will follow you – and thank you for your love and attentiveness.

A Fine Vintage
Wisterias

A Fine Vintage

If I do anything well,
it's age.

You can't drink me
except with your eyes,
but I'll flavor you
with blossom bunches galore
if you'll love me patiently,
faithfully, and prune me with vision
that lasts beyond you
and what you may see now
growing slowly
from my rough,
unrich soil…

"*Well, my wrist definitely isn't going to get any better. It really makes things difficult. I was used to just wheeling in to watch TV and then to the computer, back and forth, into the kitchen, back to the computer, etc. But now, I pretty much stay put in one spot, because it's too hard to get my hand moved onto the computer mouse or onto the remote control for the TV and back on to the wheelchair joystick, etc. It just all takes forever. Patience!*"

(e-mail from Amie)

Ornamental Grasses: Lovely Havoc

I don't love too-tame landscapes. So to add sound, rollicking texture and eccentric shapes, I enjoy using Ornamental Grasses for low-maintenance backdrop and accents in perennial gardens.

More than any others, Ornamental Grasses signify to me *freedom from rigid control*. People seem to either love or hate such plants. Some insist on calling them weeds – well, they're not, though they are tough and rowdy. They can self-seed and pop up in unexpected places, and in general, they look loose and unmanicured.

Ornamental Grasses require little maintenance; they need only to be cut down in Spring or Fall. And yet strangely (to me) many people who seek low-maintenance gardens also tend to be perfectionists about how they want their gardens ordered. Since they want their landscapes to look "less weedy," they won't let me use Ornamental Grasses in their designs, even when these would add much beauty and delight.

Ah, but nothing gives a garden more fluid movement and music than Ornamental Grasses! Some days when I'm at my office and need a break or just a lift in spirits, I go sit out near our flowing water feature, and just let the grasses' rustling there drift my better senses away into serenity.

So here's my caution: If you don't want to risk a touch or two of wildness in your garden, don't turn me loose in it!

Whispering in Wonderland

We knew a girl named Alice once
who sat down with us
to listen to the gossip
the wind whispered:

How Boxwood made Hydrangea
his mistress and Crocosima played
the devil in Spiny Bears' Britches
and Sedums taunted Rhododendrons
about mortality.

Our Northern Sea Oats played
hypocrites with thin, praying hands
holding "bread," while over Dwarf
Fountain's hedgehog heads burst
Maiden Grasses' green "fireworks."

Have any tidbits to share with us?
We'd never betray your trust,
would we?

"Controllers"

Have you ever been around "controlling" people? I mean the kind who'd never leave a few clothes on the floor or neglect chores now and then to take lovely walks on Spring days?

Some people have "control" issues with almost every plant that grows. One person I dealt with liked a certain plant's leaves but feared they'd get too big. I've heard from potential clients:

"Too bad you can't get that plant in another color…" "I like this one's shape, but its needles are prickly, so it's out…" "That flower's nice, but I just know it'll flop when it rains…" "That plant? I've seen it in other yards, so I can't have it mine… etc., etc., etc."

I confess that I find such people so draining, I'm tempted never to want to see them again.

Whenever I have to work with potential clients like these, I find that they almost never want plants that creep, self-seed, weep and/or look fluffy or might spread in any way. They always raise quick eyebrows when I mention groundcovers and say, "Oh, they won't take over the yard, will they?"

To allay their fear I try to reassure them: "These plants spread by clumping; they're non-invasive." But I can't help wondering silently: *What's at the heart of this compulsion to tightly control plants?* I know people want their gardens to look tidy, but what drives some people to obsess about even one offending tree branch that might grow beyond the reach of others and "destroy the tree's symmetry?"

All throughout history, humankind's tried to control Nature, and these days we're reaping catastrophic outcomes of cultivating too many "manicured" lawns that deplete our limited water supplies, and we're eliminating Nature's habitats for wildlife by mowing and bush-hogging every square inch of open grassy areas.

And as I write I'm thinking of more than just plants – I think about how some other people reject friends because they're going through emotional problems or are sick and in need of tending. How often people reject others outside their socioeconomic levels or because of their appearances! Those who do might miss out on the beauty of seeing beyond the fleeting flaws in themselves and others, to something much deeper: the essences of self-actualized persons or plants that are the precious products of time, attention, and healing.

Let the madness stop, I say! Let's embrace, at least in a limited way, an ornamental grass or a perennial that droops. Let the dishes stay in the sink for a day; they won't kill us. Better yet, let's admire the non-"tailored" places and people of the world and realize that all our controlling can never equal the splendor Nature Herself can create and display.

When I design landscapes, I find I can fall so short of Her when I seek to replicate her too closely. I'm saddened, too, when someone buys a wooded lot for its beauty and then cuts down most of the trees and removes all the saplings because they make the lot "look unkempt"! They're *woods* – woods are supposed to look untidy! Let the leaves fall, and get a lawn mower that can mulch them! Millions of things Nature wreathes to Her own devices are healthier and more beautiful than any we can shape with our own hands.

If you think about what else than humans uses the land and plants, it's easy to allow for some softness in your life and personal environment. Step away from the shears and let the plants grow a bit. Use natural or organic pest control methodology. (Many of today's common pesticides are non-specific and unintentionally kill beneficial insects such as honeybees; I try not to use those.)

Control issues extend to much larger environments than just your yard: Compounded, they affect the entire Earth. Look at your landscape as not just one lot in a subdivision, but as a possible stepping-stone in a migration pattern for a small group of animals. Birds might like an Ornamental Grass as a food source in Winter or use stray leaves to make a nest. If you can view things this way, you'll forget you ever thought your landscape looked scraggly or unkempt; and you'll know so much greater joy as you watch how the birds and animals take advantage of the bounty you've created.

Do you ever look in the mirror and find yourself focusing mostly on your flaws? Do you notice you've gained a few pounds, or that your hair may be getting gray? Or do you see first and foremost the beauty that resides within you as a unique individual? When I look at myself in the mirror, I don't linger over the scar I got on my face from a childhood accident; it's long become a part of my life story and me.

I love when I show up on a job with a tree or a plant that doesn't exactly match another one there, and the homeowner thinks it's the wrong variety. Once I replaced a dead hemlock with a new tree that didn't look just like the trees originally planted. The replacement tree had only a "one percent" variable difference, and a slightly more natural appearance because it came from a different supplier.

I explained that the new tree was the correct species, and that as the trees matured they'd grow to look more similar, but the client cried: "Why can't you get one that matches right now? Why are these two slightly different?"

And I thought, *How ridiculous that comment would be if we were discussing people? Do we complain that everyone is unique and possesses distinctly individual qualities?*

I love the tree that has a branch that leans to one side and isn't exactly symmetrical. I'll use it near a water feature to frame the view.

I love to walk people around my landscape nursery and show them a mound I've created out of rejected plants. I say, "There's an evergreen that used to have weak branches at its base. See that shrub? It once had some brown leaves. See those massive clumps of color over there? Would you believe it – when I found them they were perennials rejected because they 'looked weak' and 'weren't thriving!'"

People gasp in wonder at the plants I point out because they're now so thriving and magnificent, and have no apparent weaknesses. People can't believe anyone would have rejected plants that have become so near perfect.

But I don't haggle much with people over plants they don't think are quite "right." I do ask them to give the plants a chance to recover. Most will give them that chance, but others insist on immediately flawless appearances.

Let's just say that though I want very much to please my clients, if you want all neat-and-tidy, limited-color landscapes, I may give them to you (and not have much fun doing it), but I'll try before I do to persuade you to consider a natural ambience that's more adventurous, varied, meditative, playful, multi-hued – and less… well, "controlled."

Call me a "wilder" designer, but that's the way Nature made me, and I hope you have a streak of wildness in your make-up, too, that takes you "out of control" now and then!

"My tachycardia has been really bothering me for the past two weeks. Every once in a while it just feels like my heart jumps into my throat for a couple of seconds. I think it may be starting to calm down finally. The two weeks before that started, I was having horrible dizzy spells. Sometimes I could hardly sit up. And when I would lie down or get up, it felt like the entire room would totally spin out of control.

"Not to mention the horrible night sweats. I guess that's probably a hormonal thing. Then, all day I'm either freezing or burning up, yet my hands are always like ice.

"Well, I hope your day's going better than mine."

(e-mail from Amie)

Hydrangeas: Work and Reward

I'm looking over some Hydrangeas right now. You'd be amazed how many complaints like this I get about newly-planted ones: "They're wilting… and I watered them faithfully!"

"Are you sure?" I say. I find that people may swear they've watered them enough, but I know they very likely haven't. People whose Hydrangeas are failing were often first drawn to the plants' *obvious* beauty. These folks craved vast amounts of color year-long, but often they didn't bargain for the immediate and constant watering care Hydrangeas require.

But to me Hydrangeas exemplify the uniting of work and reward. With them, a little bit of work can garner you huge rewards. You need to keep in mind that the root-word in Hydrangea is *hydro*, which means *water*! If you miss even one watering on a hot day, your Hydrangea can die. But tell some people that they might need to water this plant twice a day, morning and evening, and you'd think they heard that their dog just died!

Hydrangea species include literally dozens of varieties, sizes, shapes and bloom times. Admired as they are for their romantic qualities, I prefer to look at them as just beautiful plants that are almost fool-proof in the garden — so long as you keep 'em watered well.

So for beauty worth careful nurture, by all means plant Hydrangeas! And if you want to enjoy "mopheads" like hordes of Nature's cheerleaders shaking pom-poms, or marvel at lace-caps pretty as Queen Elizabeth I's most elaborate cowls, don't miss watering these marvelous plants, for even a day.

A Hydrangea Shares Her Nightmare with Her Sister

"Dear, you look shaky
this morning – what's wrong?"

"I had the most horrible dream:
I was in an absolutely dry place
where the sun hammered
my skin without mercy,
and around me were only
fleshless animal bones
and in the distance a few
tall, green, prickly-armed plants…"

"How terrifying…"

"But that wasn't the worst part:
Beneath me spread only sand,
and no matter how deeply
I stretched my roots, they found
no water whatsoever, and I
felt myself parched and wilting…"

"My! Thank goodness that was
only a dream, and our owner keeps
us watered so well – so Dear,
just let the wind shake
your pom-poms and forget about it…"

"Oh, I wish I could – but I can't!"

"Wow! I didn't know you started writing a book! I would love to read it! Could you e-mail me a couple of passages? I think that is an incredible idea! As I said before, writing can be so cathartic…it's definitely my escape from the world. I love to sit down when the inspiration hits me and jot down things like the Magnolia Principle.

"It's just so funny how the world at large views Nature. They make the most insane comments that shed so much light onto their perceptions of life, and their personal quirks. But I have one client who talks about Nature with such joy and reverence, and has such a nurturing spirit. They're also the same folks that have fresh Chai tea and cookies made for me when I show up at their house for a Saturday appointment.

"Have a great day!"

(e-mail from Cheryl)

"Alibiers"

When it comes to caring for plants, Nature accepts no alibis. If you're not watering them correctly or keeping them in the proper light conditions, She'll tell you without fail by how badly the plants are faring.

As a landscape designer, even I have had to fess up now and then to treating plants improperly. I've tried pushing boundaries and experimenting with handling certain plants differently than Nature's blueprints, only to discover those plants' limitations the hard way, at the plants' expense. That they didn't flourish wasn't the plants fault; it was mine, for not attending rightly to their needs.

When I install a landscape I have so much to consider: plant locations, soil types, light conditions, aesthetic appeal – but most importantly of all, the landscape's future care, while and until it's getting healthfully established.

To ensure a landscape's success, you have to commit the necessary time, care and energy it needs. Watering is always a prime concern, and many of my clients want to install irrigation systems so they can avoid the work of watering. I tell them, "Irrigation's great for lawns, but not necessarily for all of a landscape's intricate and different plantings, because the plants may have many different watering requirements."

For example, evergreens in the Midwest need much less water than, say, Hydrangeas, which might sometimes need watering twice a day. On the other hand, our tight soils here can often trap moisture, and irrigation systems can sometimes actually drown plants by giving them too much water. Large trees may need deep root-watering their first season, until their vital roots are staunchly settled.

It's typical for us landscape contractors to guarantee our planting installation workmanship – *provided the plants are properly cared for, especially during certain critical time frames*. When we finish putting in a new landscape, we present the homeowner with a maintenance sheet that contains very detailed sets of watering and other requirements.

Most of my clients realize that they've made huge investments in their landscape and get excited about becoming their caretakers.

But sadly, there are always a few exceptions.

Some think the guarantee itself is an insurance policy against fatalities, and they neglect the plants, as if the guarantee can care for them without any human assistance. Then, not long after installation they call me to report inevitable symptoms of neglect such as yellowing or wilting leaves, and when I ask them if they've watered and otherwise cared for the plants according to the maintenance sheet, they'll swear up and down that they've followed the guidelines rigorously (often despite all physical evidence to the contrary).

I think of such folks as *Alibiers*. Let me tell you about one of 'em:

We designed a large commercial project in Brownsburg, Indiana, for a subdivision; as part of the installation, we planted well over 100 trees in the heat of Summer. I coordinated a way to water the trees from the subdivision's retention pond; I even trained their in-house maintenance supervisor about how long and how often to water the trees. I stressed that missing even one day could kill or severely damage them.

Two days later, I decided to stop by and see how the project was looking. Imagine my surprise and grief when I found that at least one-third of the trees were in the process of defoliating due to lack of water! I grabbed my cell phone and feigned a casual conversation with the builder to "check up on" how the trees were faring in the summer heat. He said, "Oh, fine. In fact, I've got someone out there watering them even as we speak."

I said, "Well, I'm standing at the site, and there's no one here at the moment."

After a long pause he hemmed and hawed and then said: "Uh, I didn't think missing just one day of watering would really matter."

I admit I scolded him a bit. "You wouldn't skip a day feeding or giving water to your children, would you?" I'm pleased to say that, his alibi blown, he mended his ways.

I once sold several hundred dollars worth of plants to a retail client whose house happened to be on my route home from work. I drove by day after day and saw the plants baking and shriveling in the sun, with no hose in sight. I knew the client would inevitably call and wonder why the plants had died.

I stopped at the home several times to warn that watering was imperative but never found anyone there. Sure enough, that phone call did come, with accusations that I'd sold them "non-hardy" plants. They didn't want to take responsibility for the outcome of their neglect.

Alibiers.

Amie reminds me of how much alibi-ing seems like a metaphor for life. Our relationships with friends and family can atrophy like plants do, and we can blame everyone but ourselves for not tending to those others' needs. Plants just show some of the signs of neglect more quickly than people do.

But there's a positive side to this lesson: Tending well to things other than yourself and seeing them flourish can be intensely gratifying. Once you get past alibis like, "Well, I don't know how, but it just died," or, "I didn't do anything wrong; I guess the thing just wasn't strong enough" – then you can get down to real issues of problem-solving, of plant-growing and of relationships.

With plants, when things go wrong I like to start by analyzing the soil, 'cause nine times out of ten, difficult issues start from the ground up. By process of elimination and by addressing the symptoms a plant exhibits, you can arrest the problem and save the plant.

How often in life do we get entrenched in unhealthy behaviors by creating alibis that keep us safe in our belief that "we've done nothing wrong"? Often, unhealthy alibis keep people from making healthy life choices. Landscaping and Nature can be great helpers to overcome those temptations to say, "Nothing in my life as it exists now is my fault." If you planted it – a flower or a behavior – and it's not doing well, then you may well have only you to blame. But if they thrive, you can come to know no greater joy and no greater pride as rewards for the love and care you've given.

Boxwood (Buxus Species): The Sturdy Helpers

I like to think the sturdy **"Buxus" Boxwood** makes a jolly companion for Hydrangeas, because Boxwoods protect flighty Hydrangeas from flopping and splaying in rainstorms like bedraggled teeny-boppers. If you surround your Hydrangeas with low-growing Boxwoods, the Boxwoods will act as natural staking devices.

Boxwood hedges are dense, but when I trim them I keep the electric clippers in my tool box and go at them by hand. You see, I love to fancy myself a bonsai master enjoying the feel of every cut. It's a way like none better for me to enter a calming, meditative "alpha" spirit.

Trimming a Boxwood hedge throughout the year is a great way to escape into another world; before you know it this purposeful physical exertion just seems to make the hours and stress disappear.

I find pleasing uses for Boxwoods as both a maintenance time saver, and as an opportunity to encourage people to get outside and maintain their yards (and selves!).

Boxwoods can also help hide the not-so-great looking stems of perennials such as large Phlox, Foxglove, Russian Sage, and even Ornamental Grasses. But you really should trim them once or twice a year — even three times if you're especially neatness-motivated.

My Turn for Some TLC!

Day by day I stand stout
and tall, reassuring those scaredy-
kitty Hydrangeas and covering up
the sins of low-growing soil denizens,
always the responsible one, I…

But today I get *my* treat:
My owner's trimming my hair
and I bask in the grace of
her hands as she shapes me
gentle clip by clip.

I sing silently at her
from my roots…
as she hums aloud
so softly to *me*…

"Well, all I had to do was read your note to get the tears rolling! It's nice to know someone is thinking about me! When you're stuck at home day after day, never going out or doing anything (more so in the Wintertime, because I get out more when it's warm outside) or seeing anyone¸ it's easy to feel forgotten.

"I e-mail some friends and I might hear back from them within the week; they're just too busy to answer sooner. Jen works and doesn't have email. She's always busy running her kids around after school, so it's hard to get hold of her. She usually does get hold of me over Christmas break and again in the Summertime.

"So you're the only one who always e-mails, calls or stops by to see me. And I know I can look forward to your scraping a couple of hours together to stop by for some coffee and chit-chat. Your constant and loving support means so much to me…"

(e-mail from Amie)

Spiny Bears' Britches: Not for the Faint-Hearted

These prickly plants are definitely for the open-minded. Some people think of them as "weedy," but they've got this huge plus: They're one dish rabbits have no taste for.

I've found it remarkable how often artists throughout history – from Egyptian hieroglyphists to Medieval illuminators to contemporary architectural building detailers – have admired Spiny Bears' Britches and included depictions of them in their work. So do I, whenever I can sneak them into one of my landscape-weavings!

Spiny Bears' Britches look like giant thistles, but unlike thistles they thrive in shady locations. They bloom in late Spring and amaze you with their intense, upright spikes of purple and pink, paper-like bracketed flowers. They marry well with other shady plants, acting as deep-green backdrop that helps accentuate the white flowers of Astilbe, variegated Solomon's Seal and even Lungwort (Pulmonaria).

But Spiny Bears' Britches are not for the faint of heart. Because they resemble thistles, people first seeing them say either, "Wow! That's the most unusual shade-tolerant plant I've ever seen!" or they say, "My God, I've tried for three years to get rid of thistles in my planting beds – why would I want these things anywhere near my house?"

People who harshly judge this plant also tend to dislike Sapphire Blue Sea Hollies (Eryngium "Sapphire Blue") and all the Joe Pye Weeds such as (Eupatorium dubium "Little Joe", Eupatorium fistulosum "Gateway" and Eupatorium rugosum "Chocolate"), for these, too, suffer from the "looks like a weed" syndrome.

But I love all these plants, and when I find people with truly adventurous minds, I'll sneak something like Spiny Bears' Britches into their projects. And you know what? They always tell me later that it turned out to be their favorite plant.

Why? Because Spiny Bears' Britches and most of the rest of these cultivars are *survivors*. They live in dry, tough conditions, much as weeds do, with little or no care. They also dry nicely (for decoration) and provide much-needed food (but not for rabbits) and Winter habitat for wildlife.

With Spiny Bears' Britches, then, you get so much more than just "grin-and-bear-it" marauders in your garden if you're strong enough of heart to try them!

Thinkers

Ever meet a deep-thinking rabbit?
No? Didn't figure you had.
'Cause they don't think much,
they don't like the likes of us — only
the thinkingest people do.

It takes hard thinkers to know
that life's gotta have its sharp points,
that you gotta be tough to survive
when things ain't always sunny and lush.

You gotta think past the dummies
who say you should get tossed
out with the weeds — and you
gotta have sense enough
to dress yourself bright now and then…
but not so gaudy so often that you'll
ever look good to stupid, hungry
bunnies!

"*I'm missing my plants and flowers from our old house! I did have a big container of tulips in bloom sitting on my kitchen table, but they've died off now. But at least I can look out the window and see the yard filled with dandelions!*

"*They look really pretty, small bright golden yellow flowers everywhere! I don't really understand why everyone hates them so much. Sure, they spread like wildfire, but so do other plants. I guess people just want their green lawns plain, with no flowers at all disturbing that plain green.*

"*So, the persistent dandelions have been tagged a weed! Have you ever had a client in your entire life who liked dandelions? Well, I do.*

"*My redbuds all have little buds of leaves on them! We planted some raspberry, blackberry and blueberry bushes around back by the garage last week. With the cold weather snap we just had, I'm glad I didn't plant any flowers. I can't wait to sell our old house and get this new yard going!*"

(e-mail from Amie)

The Lucifer Plant (Crocosmia x Lucifer)

Whenever I get a yen to "give the devil his due," I go for a sprinkling of Lucifer Plants in a landscape. Indeed, their clumps of green, sword-shaped leaves with tall, arching spikes of flame-red and funnel-shaped blossoms can make them seem like demons dancing on dragons' bones. If I find a Magnolia-Principled garden lover with a lust for the unusual, I'll eagerly offer Lucifers.

Lucifers can't be all "evil," of course – hummingbirds are known to sip at them avidly. And their tremendous, pendulous, red, orchid-like flowers appeal to just about anyone who's not turned off by their name.

I actually once snuck this plant into a design for a local church (I peered over my glasses quizzically when I told the client its common name and almost used only the scientific name so as not to jeopardize my option to use it.)

But I confess to loving this plant with more than just the "devil" in me. The Lucifer seems naturally rebellious, like me, because it looks like a tropical plant that shouldn't be able to survive in our climate, yet it mischievously does thrive, even here.

I think my grandmother knew these plants' spirit. To scare the living daylights out of me and my three siblings before we walked nights down the long gravel path back to my parents' house, she used to recite (from memory, no less) the Hoosier Poet, James Whitcomb Riley's classic "Little Orphant Annie," with its famous, ominous refrain:

> *An' the Gobble-uns'll git you*
>
> *If you*
>
> *Don't*
>
> *Watch*
>
> *Out!*

I never heard her say so, but I can't imagine Grandma not having profound, grinning affection for the devilish Lucifer Plant.

People who are Plant Collectors (see below) love the Lucifer's look, since Collectors are always on the hunt for something no one else has in their gardens. It's more unusual to find Lucifer Plants in Indiana than plants like Purple Cone Flowers. So if I know someone who dabbles with gardening and thinks they know all the plant choices, I'll whip this plant out of my bag of tricks.

I like to imagine that the Lucifer itself just proudly thinks it's among the Universe's most amazing gifts – and I think that's just about right!

Ugly? Evil? Us?

They say we're kin to zombies,
goblins 'n' ghouls, BUT... those
creepy things are all ugly and gross and wicked —
not like us, so pretty and virtuous, right?

Look at us here in our stately red row:
would **you** have kicked us out of
the Original Garden and made us
crawl on our bellies just for being wise?

Oh, you don't have to love us
(though you might well, so comely we are),
but please, do us this favor:
Don't try to imagine what
we might turn into once
dark drops down
to black out day!

"Plant Collectors"

Almost all my landscape clients come knocking on my door with one big problem:

They love plants, but they just don't know how to design a planting plan that doesn't come out looking like it was contrived or overworked. To be safe, they would tend to fall back into patterns that felt unadventurously comfortable, such as to line shrubs all together in a straight row, or just match them symmetrically. They think of planting in "barber pole" fashion, with alternating color stripes, or maybe even jam some 20 different species closely into one tight little corner of their yard. But these fall-back strategies are just symptoms of how they view the use of plant materials – primarily as sheer, simple decoration.

But they seek me out because they're not completely sure of their own judgments about landscaping. And of those who come to me, the clients I find most challenging are the ones I like to call "Plant Collectors." (I have a soft spot for them because I sometimes suspect I'm something of one myself.)

These people buy every tantalizing garden book they can find, filled with dazzling pictures that show plants in just the right settings. Plant Collectors love to ruminate over each plant selection, and they bring to my office piles of old *Wayside Garden* catalogs, painstakingly tagged with dozens of post-it notes to remind them of their favorite choices.

Don't get me wrong, I love clients who delight in contributing to the design process, but to some Plant Collectors what loom as most important are minute details rather than the bigger pictures that will be their entire gardens.

Sometimes they get exasperated if I tell them that a particular combination of individual plant characteristics isn't available, or that parts of the mix they've chosen aren't compatible with one another.

Some look at me in disbelief, acrimony and even suspicion, and they ask, "You mean there aren't any evergreen shrubs that flower orange all Summer in dense shade?" or, "Oh, you're saying I can't have that shrub grow only 24 inches tall so I never have to trim it?" and, "Wouldn't it really be nice if that plant made Fall color changes, too?"

After such discussions I've had many a silent conversation with God go like this: *Hello, God? Uh, yeah… I have a request… I know you're busy, but I'd like you to make me an evergreen shrub that flowers all summer orange, in dense shade, and only gets 24 inches tall. Oh, and if you could add in some Fall color that would be great! Yeah, I know it's a great idea, and that you should've thought of it yourself, but…*

Well, as you've probably guessed, God just smiles and kinda lets me know he's not ready to recreate his Universe just yet. And some clients have a hard time accepting that plants can't be stamped out at the flower factory to our exact specifications. (Oh, Amie, why can't they all be more like you?)

Sure, botanists are developing new cultivars all the time, but why can't we happy with what Nature's already provided for us? We have so many choices already, surely we can make some that'll be as amazing as our most creative dreams and provide season-changing interest at the same time.

So, my Plant Collector friend, can we sit down again, discard the *im*possibilities and talk over all the myriad *possible* possibilities?

"Are you enjoying the heat, or do you like it a bit cooler? I like it cooler… it's better for the plants. Hey, Ron and I went and purchased some water plants yesterday for our Fox 59 Interview on the 28th. I wish you got the local Fox station, because we'll be on at 7:45 and 8:00 a.m., I think. They'll be interviewing me first about design, then Ron about construction methodology.

"The plants we got are totally cool… one looks like a pot plant! It was in the open back of our truck all the way home, and we passed at least three cops, who all gave us the eye! We just laughed as we passed by and waved… it was too funny! I was almost hoping one of them would pull us over. Can you imagine the conversation? 'Really, Officer, it's just an aquatic plant, trust me!' We bought some beautiful water lilies, some variegated cattails and some emergent plants that float around and look like underwater grass! Totally awesome!

"You would LOVE the nursery we purchased them from – it's like a water garden HEAVEN! The sound of water was all around us, it was kind of like being at the ocean or a huge waterfall. And there were cool fish and bog plants… frogs chirping… Man, I wish you could have been with us! Maybe Ron and I could take you and the girls some time… they would LOVE to see it!

"I'll try and e-mail you some pictures of the plants!

"Love,"

(e-mail from Cheryl)

Sedums: Stubborn and Relentless!

Do you tend to be on the lazy side as a gardener? Want for part of your landscape a rock plant that's virtually unkillable? Try **Sedums**, 'cause I tell you, as they peer from between stones and sprawl out to cover ground, they epitomize resilience and relentless growth. Sedums are stubborn as all get-out to stay alive! Some folks even put them on "living roofs," and they reduce home heating and cooling costs by 20-25%.

I swear, it seems you could transport a batch of Sedums from the greenhouse to your car, and if one small branch dropped on the ground, that sucker would sprout! Sedums come in every conceivable color, shape and size, and they provide both color and texture in so many ways.

Hey, if you're lazy, why plant Mums when

you can spend your money on Sedums instead? One of my favorite Sedums is Angelina (Sedum rupestre 'Angelina'). It somewhat resembles spruce, but turns a bright golden color and then orange toward Winter.

Watch those Sedums creep between joints of patios and pathways and make a great "container" plant. And another bonus: They'll contrast wonderfully with any blue-colored perennial you might plant to complement 'em.

Plant 'em, then just try to destroy 'em – I dare ya!

Sedums
Take It from the Top!

Hey, you down there!
Know how we got up here on this roof?
We played it cool and thick.
We laid such dense carpets
on the ground, some human got
the idea to take pity on our humble
state and plant us on a home's roof!

Now we're so grateful we decided
to save that human a fortune
by being the home's blanket
so it stays warm in Winter, cool in Summer.

Who says the downtrodden
can never be exalted?

"Hey, I've been thinking a lot, and I just wanted to say that friends never really seem to get to say sincerely what we think about one another, and damn it, I don't want to get too busy and not tell you how great I think you are.

"We've been friends a long time, and through all the years I don't think I've ever heard an unkind, insincere word come out of your mouth. I always think we've made a good match…I'm 'out there' and you seem to calm me down…a quiet spirit. That's a real trick…Ron knows this, you know this…

"You look like a cute little elf, with your small nose and oval-shaped face. I've always thought you were super-beautiful…even as a teenager/dopey adolescent. Everyone who's ever met you whom I've spoken with agrees on this point…especially in high school. Even after any Christmas parties, everyone would say how cute you looked and what a cute friend I have…

"I wish we could have more times like that…just you and me together talking about silly things. Maybe we can make time to do that this year. You are the kindest and best person I've EVER known…

"Don't know why… just wanted to say all that.
"Love you much,
"C.J."

(e-mail from Cheryl)

PJM Rhododendron: Risky Beauty

*I*f I meet Indiana people who have aversion to risk and low frustration tolerance for possible garden fatalities, I caution them against planting **Rhododendrons** (and Azaleas) here in Indiana, because our soil pH tends not to be in their best flourishing range. And if I design this plant into my plans for them, I've already got my speech prepared about its best care, to allay their concerns about its survivability.

I also brag on these plants' beauty and remind folks that if they've ever turned lemons into lemonade and are willing to give these acid-loving plants proper protection, Rhododendrons will survive and lavish with peerless loveliness. I say, "It's a broad-leafed evergreen, it turns red in the Fall, and it blooms lavender in the Spring – to me this is the most beautiful combination of plant traits. What more could you ask for?" With such encouragement, I find that deeply Magnolia-Principled garden-lovers are often eager to give them a try.

Still, most of my clients shy away from using them because they think that (unlike those tough little guys, Sedums) Rhododendrons aren't hardy (though hardiness refers, really, to plants' ability to do well given the average mean temperature range in which things grow). The Rhododendron is indeed "hardy," but there's more than just cold-hardiness to be considered.

Sometimes because a person's tried a certain type of plant that's congenitally hardy once and one of the plants died, he or she gets a bias against it, and now they'll never try it again.

They'll say things like, "Those XYZ plants… they all just die." And if I try to convince them to give the plants another chance, a wall goes up and the plants never get inside it.

So Rhododendrons are just not for people who are too prone to say about any plant, "I tried one once and it died!" But give Rhododendrons what they need, and they'll survive, even Indiana's climate.

Don't you think they might be worth a planting?

Rhododendron
Why Am I So Wonderful for You?

Wonder why I thrive so well for you?
I like to be green, but I blush red in Fall
because you treat my soil just right.

Why do I try so hard to bloom
radiantly for you each Spring?
You risk my life for a vision of my beauty.

Why am I toughly tender enough
to survive Winter for you?
You love me enough to give
me what I need to love
you back all Summer!

"Why-ers"

Plant fatalities are always an issue in my business, so all plant lovers are what I call "Why-ers" from time to time. Even with the best care, 100 percent plant survivability isn't possible, so at least once or twice a week some client or other and I will have a conversation about why something died.

Generally, I go through a checklist of requirements that can help diagnose whatever problems have arisen or may arise. I first ask the client how much they're watering, for how long and if their watering seems to be within the proper range.

If I find no stumbling blocks there, I move to soil fertility. I ask them to check the pH range, the amount of drainage, and even the consistency of the soil. If these match up to the plants' requirements, I ask about the plants' location. Is the plant a "sunny" one that's been too much in the shade? Is it a plant that needs protection from Winter winds?

If I determine that all the proper requirements have been met, I move on to possible insect infestation or fungal diseases and nutritional requirements. Maybe the plant needs fertilizing, or Japanese Beetles are eating it (both are common problems in the Midwest).

My final query: Can I re-check the plant to make sure it was installed correctly? Could I maybe have planted it too deeply?

If none of those prove operative concerns, I just have to shrug, "Sorry, but I don't know what killed your plant." I can suggest that perhaps "transplant shock," a sort of failure to thrive after being moved, did the plant in. Maybe the roots got jarred in moving, or maybe an air pocket in the soil caused the plant to settle so that water collected around the roots and damaged them.

"Well," a client may say, "why did one plant die though it was planted right next to another one that thrived? They were planted with the same procedures, then they received the exact same care, watering and other physical requirements…"

"WHY?! Why, why, why..?" these folks understandably want to know. "You're the expert… the one with the degree!" they tell me. Some "Why-ers" seem especially miffed if I can't give them an exact post-mortem diagnosis.

That's when I can only ask them in return: "Why does one cancer patient die, while another who's received the exact same diagnosis, treatment and care survive?"

They can't answer that question, and neither can I.

But consider this Magnolia-Principled way of looking at the "whys": Sometimes you don't *need* to know why. Think about the plant's experience: For a tree, getting dug from an original home where it was thriving is akin to major surgery. When you begin to think about Nature's plant denizens as living entities and not just products, even the "whys" don't seem so unjust.

I sometimes think: *Why did my best friend Amie develop ALS, and why did my brother David die of leukemia?* Too many "whys?" snarl into futile tangles that can keep you from enjoying plants and people in the exact moment you inhabit now. They can keep you from just accepting that the plant died and replacing it to make room for other, new plants (or persons) life calls you to care for. Why do you need to ponder the mysteries of Fate… or Chance? Concentrate on fulfilling the needs of those around you and the plants you tend to, and you'll find joy in that facet of the Magnolia Principle.

Sometimes there just is no *why*. People can get so bogged down in questions like, "*Why* don't I have more money?" or "*Why* can't I find that special person in my life!" or "*Why* can't I let go of the past?" Oh, you should ponder your checklist and correct problems now and then, but sometimes… things just happen! You may have a bad winter that kills a few shrubs… it happens!

Things that you don't want to happen are bound to pop up; it's how you deal with their aftermath that counts. Don't let that negative loop develop in your mind that keeps you thinking about that plant that died!

Remember: *One negative incident doesn't predict all future events.* Can you join me in resisting the temptation to keep wondering over and over, *Why, why, why?* Think of the plants that survived, the moments that were good – and the future delights that await you and your garden as you both thrive from here on!

The Shrub (KnockOut) Rose

For obvious reasons, the Rose symbolizes romance. Nothing's more colorful and striking, and no flower's more likely to create a visceral response like a gasp of awe and tactile pleasure at its sheer beauty and silky petal-smoothness. Surely, once you know how to care for this plant, you'll fall hopelessly in love with it. If want to hear an, "Oh!" or an "Ah!" when you show off your garden, just steer your friends to the Roses.

Still, ravishing as they are, Roses sometimes garner complaints as well as compliments. People love them when they're blooming and hate them when they're not. Roses only bloom newly on new growth, so once a Rose plant has bloomed, you have to trim it if you want to see it bloom again. (You also have to fend off the marauding Japanese Beetles who find Roses so delicious, and that also requires some special maintenance.)

Most folks want Roses because of their color, but during the latter part of the Summer, once a plant's gone through its initial blooming, starts to develop rose-hips or seed pods and puts out some rouge branches, some people can get disappointed. When I tell them there's no problem, really, the plants just need vigorously pruning, they cock their heads to the side like parakeets listening to catch words. And they say, "Really? I thought you could damage them by pruning them too much."

"Not so," I smile, "in fact, it's just the opposite."

Shrub Roses are indeed true **KnockOuts** (their alternate name) if you treat these thorny plants right. This may sound odd, but you should leave their bushes intact (though bloomless, of course) all Winter – *then* you "knock 'em out," that is, cut them down, come Spring. New roses will "rise before the 10-count" on top of new bush growth, and you'll have to trim that new growth even once it's bloomed. As you might guess, being Roses they're lovers as well as fighters, and both qualities always seem to please us, don't they?

"Ron and I saved a chipmunk last week that got caught in a window well at a job site! He was on the brink of death and we SAVED HIM!!! We gave him water-soaked bread and named him Skipper (after the castaway/'Gilligan's Island' scenario). We really thought he was a goner, but overnight he regained his health, and we let him go in the woods!

"How's that for cheering you up! Think of Skipper out enjoying his little chipmunk life…eating nuts and burrowing in a little hole somewhere in the woods! One small step for the animal kind, one giant step for Ron and Cheryl's good deed list!!"

(e-mail from Cheryl)

Cut Me Good, Lover!

If you wanta keep me tender,
sometimes you'll treat me tough.
If you want my petals lavish,
you'll cut me good enough.

Nah, you don't have to worry
when come Spring you lay me down —
I'll rise before you know it
to spread my red around.

Don't let no beetles bite me,
but trim me when it's hot.
Stay nicely mean now, baby,
an' I'll give you all I got!

The Daylily:
Now You Have It, Now You Don't!

Which flower opens at sunrise and shrivels by sunset (yet some blossoms are replaced by others on the same stems the very next day!) – explaining its apt name? The **Daylily**, which speaks to me of time's fleeting nature and the need to live fully (and well, as Amie does) in time's given moments. Yet it seems everyone loves the poor Daylily until its blossoms are spent, leaving nothing but the foliage and a memory.

But just as we keep loving elderly folks after they've bloomed, we have a chance to keep falling in love with Daylilies again and again. They have Asian origins, and you may well unknowingly have eaten their petals in Chinese cuisine (like hot-and-sour soup

and moo shu pork). People also don't realize that there are other ways you can eat the blossoms. I love to mix them into salads. If I can convince you to take a leap of faith, you'll love the flavor. Though Daylilies don't usually give off a scent, their petals taste like sweet lettuce.

I forgot about the Daylily's nature once and tried to cut one and bring it inside to pretty things up. It was in full bloom by mid-morning, but by evening it had shrunk to nothing. Thankfully, I'd picked a branch that had more than one blossom.

Be ready to defend Daylilies against tiny but harmful enemies, most commonly, spider-mites. I like to think Daylilies teach us about the preciousness of things of beauty that may not last long, but are worth their existence for the indelible pleasure they give while they're with us.

"Hey! Well, I haven't gone to my regular doctor about the tachycardia. I'm pretty sure he would just tell me to increase the dosage of the medication I take to see if that helped. Last time I saw him, he was very surprised that the tiny dosage I took was actually working. I actually tried increasing it for a few days and it really didn't make a difference. I went back to the regular dosage and now it seems to be getting a little better, so who knows what was wrong??? I mentioned it to the doctor I get the herbal medicine for my ALS from, and she suggested I might be low on salt and that my electrolytes were off.

"See if you can set aside an hour or two one of these days to bring some Starbucks and sit and talk. Or come by without the Starbucks; it's not a requirement for coming to visit, ha ha!

"Oh, I should tell you that I know what I'm getting you for your birthday! It's on the 15th, right? I'm terrible with dates lately. The theme for your gift is 'favorites.'"

(e-mail from Amie)

See You Tomorrow?

Yes, I confess I'm shrinking
and curling up on you tonight;
sorry, it's just the way I am —
can you live with that?

I know, you wish tender and dainty
things could last forever, but
nothing does, really, even rocks
crumble, iron rusts, glass melts,
empires, like the Chinese dynasties
that birthed me, corrupt and collapse.

Yet no true loveliness, even mine,
can vanish for always.
So, rather than toss me aside,
can you keep me and have faith my blossoms
will return for you tomorrow
when you wake? I hope I'll see you
then — if you'll wake, too…
May I believe you will?

Indian Pink (*Spigelia marilandica*): Good, Wild "Medicine"

To me, Indian Pinks represent the whole range of native American species that go under-appreciated by people who feel compelled to try "manicuring" the world. But I guarantee you: One look at this plant and you'll want these Native Americans to make a comeback that'll suffuse all our boring yards with excitement.

Do *you* ever get the urge to "manicure" the world? If so, you might not want **Indian Pinks** in your garden, but to me (and hummingbirds, too, 'cause they delight in Indian Pinks' nectar) they sum up all that's wild and beautiful in Nature, like Native Americans chanting rhythmically in full ornamental regalia, white headdresses and ceremonial necklaces, their little red tubular blossoms are to die for.

Native Americans once found their roots "good medicine," too, for a variety of ills. I long to invite them to Powow wherever a Magnolia-Principled gardener will let me.

Powwow

Come, sit by the fire
and share this pipe with us.
Take the little smoke in deep
and see if you agree:

Haven't the ones with pale minds
gambled **with** our land long enough?
Isn't it just, then, that now
they've come **on** our land to wager?

As darkness starts to fall, will you
wait with us, until their last
bet on the wrong number tests the wheel
and they lose our land back to us?

Then, as the light dims, you'll come dance
and chant with us the flutter and spark
of the hummingbirds' return!

"*I know what you mean, I just think it's very difficult for most people to see themselves with much clarity. It's hard to really analyze yourself and take the tough steps necessary to improve your life.*

"*Changing destructive life patterns takes work, and to do it you can't be physically, emotionally and spiritually lazy. Look at how many people are overweight and take drugs. Look at how many people have tortured relationships and broken families. And look at how apathetic so many people are toward each other's struggles.*

"*Why? Because eating healthy and exercising take work. Because admitting you're wrong every once in a while and forging healthy relationships isn't easy. Because caring about someone else takes effort. It's a hard road toward personal enlightenment. People want to write this little story in which they're the star and can do no wrong. I really, truly believe that to some extent, most people care about others, but certain people only wallow in these false stories of their lives. I think the truth and the change would be too much to overcome for most.*"

(e-mail from Cheryl)

Weeds, Weeds, Go Away!

*I*nevitably I find Weeds rousting their way into my tangle of weaving threads. Uppity and demanding attention, they remind me personally that we live in a universe that, even while some of it evolves, it also *de*volves by inexorable Law (Newton's Second of Thermodynamics, no less), from order to disorder.

I confess that I like to find a few weeds' presences in some unexpected natural contexts – "happy accidents" of sorts – and when I do, I'm tempted to rewrite the rules of landscaping to create new exceptions that allow us ways to "hug" those weeds now and then.

I'm only half sorry to say: No magic bullet exists that will eliminate weeds entirely from the world or your garden. Make war on them how you will, weeds will persist.

I wish I could show you the looks on some of my clients' faces when I break that news to them. Some tell me pleadingly, "You're saying that with all of today's technological advancements, they still haven't developed products that can do away with *weeds*?"

I answer, "Well, you can buy some things that will help keep weeds at bay. But nothing you can buy fully protects all plants from all weeds. It's like in life: You can take all the vitamins in the world, eat right, get great nights' sleep, yet you can still get sick. Germs and viruses happen!

"So do weeds."

Ralph Waldo Emerson once said, "A weed is a plant whose virtues have yet to be discovered." An amazing statement, huh? What makes something a weed, really? Our own personal assessment of a particular plant's value or lack of it. (Many farmers here in the Midwest mow down areas that look "weedy," but quite often to the detriment of wildlife that then has to struggle for grassy cover and migration corridors.) Interesting, isn't it, how we give worth-assessments to living entities, declaring some beautiful and others ugly?

I strongly suspect that our attitudes toward weeds also reflect our internal struggles to deal with imperfections of all kinds in our lives.

Sometimes people's attitudes toward glitches in things can be real head-scratchers. Not long ago I was working on a new home in an elite Carmel, Indiana, neighborhood, and the homeowner proudly escorted me through the finished rooms. The interior and exterior centered around recreating Tuscan "vernacular" themes, including woodwork that appeared well-worn and plaster that looked as if it were crumbling.

But whenever we stepped on a single floorboard that uttered the slightest squeak, the owner would tell me about how disappointed she was to own a new house with a creaking floor and other such incongruities here and there.

I asked her curiously, "What is it about Tuscan landscapes that you admire most?" She waxed warmly about Tuscany's well-worn paths and soft natural landscapes and how the old buildings there had so much character, and how she was trying to emulate that in her new home.

Ironically, though, without any real *weathering or squeaks,* I thought.

Of course, the issue of perceived imperfection spills over into many facets of my profession. These days we build, for instance, patios using many different kinds of materials, such as bluestone and brick, but I've noticed that the more natural, less "orderly" materials have fallen out of favor of late.

I see a continued trend toward installing concrete block walls and paving slabs, perhaps because they have very tight, consistent tolerances. Each block and slab is exactly the same thickness. Unlike them, bluestone varies in size and thickness. If stones you use differ in thicknesses and shapes, it's harder to set them down levelly and regularly.

But don't we all, at least secretly, crave certain amounts of "happy imperfection" in our lives?

People pursue happiness in many different ways. It seems, though, that a large segment of the population thinks eliminating all imperfections – in their appearances, their homes, children, cars, friends and elsewhere – will make them happy. But they don't seem to realize that once they've eliminated one imperfection, they'll just find another. Infinite "perfection" in this world is an illusion.

To me, true joy in gardening includes appreciation and acceptance of weeds, those critters that don't exist to offend, but just exist to *be*.

Most people do hate weeds, and especially weeding by hand.

Me? I find weeding meditative. I don't have to focus sharply while I do it, and I can be gaily surprised by joyous anomalies along the way. Such as: I love when a stray Purple Cone Flower self-seeds into my gravel pathway and takes root. I adore when my Japanese Blood Grass co-mingles with my Blue Rug Juniper to create a blurred line of contrast and color. Nothing thrills me more than to return to a job site I installed over three years ago, and see that all the mulch has disappeared and given way to drifts of soft, weedy plant materials that have turned the site to look like a pastoral painting.

Have you ever tried to grasp that weeds *are* going to happen, that concrete *is* going to crack, and stone patios *will* settle? What's wrong with inevitable evolution like this? If Nature always

tends toward disorder, and it takes countering energy to keep things in order, where happiness lies, I think, is in cultivating a symbiotic relationship between *re*ordering processes and chores and appreciating life's and Nature's happy miscues.

When I chat with Amie about people's mad pursuit of control and elimination of all imperfection, she just sighs. Almost every day, she lacks control to watch what she wants to on TV – or even to feed herself. Yet she's learned to enjoy the surprises of being *out* of control – and she's helped teach me that same kind of joy.

It's a way of thinking, feeling and being that can spill over into so many corners of your life. This way you appreciate the unique qualities your friends and plants possess, rather than magnifying their faults or how you "wish they were."

I have clients who love almost all plants, and when I explain to them why a particular characteristic of a plant restricts its use in the design we're discussing, they accept this with very little fuss.

Amie's that kind of person. I so admired her calm acceptance of her illness when she was diagnosed. And I doubt that I'd be as tolerant as she's been of the life changes she's endured without anger and impatience.

When she first learned she'd contracted ALS, you wouldn't have known there was anything wrong with her, though you might have noticed her occasional stumble, and she'd report a fall now and then that resulted in a minor bruise.

But soon when she walked across a room she needed an arm to grab hold of, and at last she had to resort to a wheelchair. As close friends we often share now about her daily challenges and how she has to accept and adjust to each new incapacity her body experiences and learn to maximize her gratitude for what she still has – the day's mobility and more – even while she must consider realistically what she might not have or be able to do tomorrow.

We laugh about how beautiful, varied and enlightening Nature can be when She's treated right, and how people should release, accept and enjoy their lives and all She gives them.

Just recently Amie e-mailed me: "A bit of good news today: When I try to get my hand onto the joystick of my wheelchair, I actually can do it. I guess maybe it's going to be something I can or can't do from now on, depending on my energy level or how I'm feeling each day. But at least I can do it part of the time!"

"Weeds" of her life and all, I'd say Amie's lives all the life she has, all the time!

Shouldn't we all?

"Hi, there! Well, I'll say again: You are the absolute best friend in the world, hands down, no contest! You always make me laugh! And you always understand me. We think a lot alike. I still sometimes think we're the only normal people out there, everyone else is crazy! I think we were meant to be best friends.

"I didn't get the best parents in the world, and overall, I had a really crappy childhood. But so what? I believe that we all choose our families before we're born, for the lessons we'll learn from those families. That's the only sense I can make of it all. And I chose you before you were or I were born, and you became a bright light in my life.

"I'm glad if you think I've helped you in any way. I never get tired of talking to you about anything… whether it's something exciting in your life, or your problems just existing. I think we could go on for days before we ran out of things to talk about. And I hope you never feel like your problems are not as important or as huge as mine."

(e-mail from Amie)

Near Ready to Open...

Now to draw these diverse threads together, water them with a fountain, illumine them with this fire pit emblazoned with a cast-iron silhouette of a Magnolia Tree, and do some final arranging…

I'm done weaving now; soon the doors to the Show will open, and hopefully before the day's out I'll embrace a new cadre of Magnolia-Principled friends, and renew old friendships, too, like Amie's, because she always finds a way to attend my shows and share with me Nature's colors and forms so strong they stick forever to our senses!

Thanks so much for joining us!

fire-builder's epitaph

i am the slow fire-builder under ground
covered with stones and soil my body rests
my hands blaze wild grass shoots into wind

my hair's sown with sedums my mouth opens
i smile lucifers and take acorns for eyes
between my thighs a thick-furred boxwood sleeps

from my breasts burn roses' tongues
bears' britches and weeds scratch me
to ashes hydrangeas hatch in my toes
i'm dressed in daylilies steeped
in water craved above seeped below
over the rock on which i lie

my thoughts are wisterias' dreams
indian pinks' roots
rhododendrons' lust for sun

scorched by such life, my bones will not be found
i am the slow fire-builder under ground...

Acknowledgments:

Thanks to Hortech, Inc. of Nunica, Michigan for allowing me to incorporate their amazing photographs. Your catalogs, and website information have inspired my landscape master plans for countless years. I've pored over your imagery to gain much needed insight, inspiration and horticultural knowledge.

Thanks to Nicholas Marco for your constant encouragement, editing, rewriting, help with the lovely poetry, and the necessary gardener's spirit that helped coax this blossom of writer's hope.

Thanks also to Amie Thornburg for allowing me to share our most private conversational moments. I hope they give the inspiration of hope and acceptance for so many future gardeners. Your constant spirit in light of such adversity allowed me to see and experience a greater awakening in myself.

Picture Credits:

Hortech, Inc.
14109 Cleveland Street
Nunica, Michigan 49448
www.premiumplants.net

Photographer: Dave MacKenzie
Crocosmia x Lucifer   45
Double Knock Out Rose   62
Eringium 'Saphire Blue'   40
Japanese Blood Grass   74
Northern Sea Oats   20
Spigelia Miratlantica   68
Spiny Bears Britches (image of leaves)   39
Spiny Bears Britches (image of flower)   41
Strawberry Candy Daylily   63
Summer Wine Daylily   66
Wisteria 'Amethyst Falls'   14
Wisteria 'Honbeni'   16

Dreamstime (Copyright Free Images)
www.dreamstime.com

Photographer: Liliya Zakharchenko
Basil in Pots   9
Photographer: www.rinusbaakphotography.com
Chipmunk   61
Photographer: Serban Enache
Cover Image
Photographer: www.ciogiart.com
Dandilions   42
Photographer: www.dreamstime.com
Forest Fire   78
Photographer: Steffens Steffens
Magnolia Bud   11
Photographer: Ruta Saulyte
Rhodendron   55
Photographer: Karoline Cullen
Sculpted Boxwood   37
Photographer: www.callessienaturephotography.com
Weed   70
Photographer: Serg Myshkovvsky
Wet Magnolia   13
Photographer: Takeshi Nishio
Wisteria Leaf   17

Brower/Jacques Design, Inc.
1944 North 500 East
Greenfield, Indiana 46140
www.browerjacques.com
(317) 462-7557

Photographers: Ron and Cheryl Jacques
Adagio Grass   72
Amie and Cheryl   iii
Aquatic Plants   48
Back Cover
Black Eyed Susan   30
Boxwood   35
Brick Arch   76
Creeping Thyme   21
Edmondson Residence waterfall   18
Edmondson Residence water feature   38
Fall Magnolia   6
Hydrangea   29
Leaves in Water   26
Ornamental Grass Explosion   19
Parents Nursery   2
Rooftop Sedum   49
Sedum   51
Stone Patio   73
Tuscan Garden   viii
Tuscan Garden 2   3
White Cone Flower   52
Winter Grasses   69
Winter Scene   65
Wall Fountain   23
White Hydrangea   28

LaVergne, TN USA
02 March 2010
174630LV00001B